BASSAI SHO, KANKŪ SHO, CHINTE

BEST KARATE 9

Bassai Sho. Kankū Sho. Chinte

M. Nakayama

KODANSHA INTERNATIONAL

Tokyo and New York

Kata in this volume demonstrated by Takeshi Ōishi, Keigo Abe and Mikio Yahara, instructors of the Japan Karate Association.

Front cover photo by Keizō Kaneko.

Distributed in the United States by Kodansha International/USA Ltd., through Harper & Row, Publishers, Inc., 10 East 53rd Street, New York, New York 10022.

Published by Kodansha International Ltd., 2-2 Otowa 1-chome, Bunkyo-ku, Tokyo 112 and Kodansha International/USA Ltd., 10 East 53rd Street, New York, New York 10022. Copyright © 1985 by Kodansha International Ltd. All rights reserved. Printed in Japan.
LCC 77-74829
ISBN 0-87011-680-0
ISBN 4-7700-1180-6 (in Japan)

First edition, 1985
Third printing, 1988

CONTENTS

Dedicated
to my teacher
GICHIN FUNAKOSHI

INTRODUCTION

The past decades have seen a great increase in the popularity of karate-dō throughout the world. Among those who have been attracted to it are college students and teachers, artists, businessmen and civil servants. It has come to be practiced by policemen and members of Japan's Self-defense Forces. In a number of universities, it has become a compulsory subject, and that number is increasing yearly.

Along with the increase in popularity, there have been certain unfortunate and regrettable interpretations and performances. For one thing, karate has been confused with the so-called Chinese-style boxing, and its relationship with the original Okinawan *Te* has not been sufficiently understood. There are also people who have regarded it as a mere show, in which two men attack each other savagely, or the contestants battle each other as though it were a form of boxing in which the feet are used, or a man shows off his talent for breaking bricks or tiles with his head, hand or foot.

If karate is practiced solely as a fighting technique, this is cause for regret. The fundamental techniques have been developed and perfected through long years of study and practice, but to make any effective use of these techniques, the spiritual aspect of this art of self-defense must be recognized and must play the predominant role. It is gratifying to me to see that there are those who understand this, who know that karate-dō is a purely Oriental martial art, and who train with the proper attitude.

To be capable of inflicting devastating damage on an opponent with one blow of the fist or a single kick has indeed been the objective of this Okinawan martial art. But even the practitioners of old placed stronger emphasis on the spiritual side of the art than on the techniques. Training means training of body and spirit, and, above all else, one should treat his opponent courteously and with the proper etiquette. It is not enough to fight with all one's power; the real objective in karate-dō is to do so for the sake of justice.

Gichin Funakoshi, a great master of karate-dō, pointed out repeatedly that the first purpose in pursuing this art is the nurturing of a sublime spirit, a spirit of humility. Simultaneously, a power sufficient to destroy a ferocious wild animal with a single blow should be developed. Becoming a true follower of karate-dō is possible only when one attains perfection in these two aspects, the one spiritual, the other physical.

Karate as an art of self-defense and karate as a means of improving and maintaining health has long existed. During the past twenty years, a new activity has been explored and is coming to the fore. This is *sports karate.*

In sports karate, contests are held for the purpose of determining the ability of the participants. This needs emphasizing, for here again there is cause for regret. There is a tendency to be too concerned about winning contests, and those who do so neglect the practice of fundamental techniques, opting instead to attempt jiyū kumite at the earliest opportunity.

Stress on winning contests cannot help but alter the fundamental techniques a person uses and the practice he engages in. Not only that, it will result in a person's being incapable of executing a strong and effective technique, which, after all, is the unique characteristic of karate-dō. The man who begins jiyū kumite prematurely—without sufficient practice of fundamentals—will soon be surpassed by the man who has trained in the basic techniques long and diligently. It is, quite simply, a case of haste makes waste. There is no alternative to learning and practicing basic techniques and movements step by step, stage by stage.

If karate competitions are to be held, they must be conducted under suitable conditions and in the proper spirit. The desire to win a contest is counterproductive, since it leads to a lack of seriousness in learning the fundamentals. Moreover, aiming for a savage display of strength and power in a contest is totally undesirable. When this happens, courtesy toward the opponent, which is of first importance in any expression of karate, is forgotten. I believe this matter deserves a great deal of reflection and self-examination on the part of both instructors and students.

To explain the many and complex movements of the body, it has been my desire to present a fully illustrated, up-to-date text, based on the experience in this art that I have acquired over a period of five decades. This hope is being realized by the publication of the *Best Karate* series, in which earlier writings of mine have been totally revised with the help and encouragement of my readers. This new series explains in detail what karate-dō is in language made as simple as possible, and I sincerely hope that it will be of help to followers of karate-dō. I hope also that karateka in many countries will be able to understand each other better through this series of books.

WHAT KARATE-DŌ IS

Deciding who is the winner and who is the loser is not the ultimate objective. Karate-dō is a martial art for the development of character through training, so that the karateka can surmount any obstacle, tangible or intangible.

Karate-dō is an empty-handed art of self-defense in which the arms and legs are systematically trained and an enemy attacking by surprise can be controlled by a demonstration of strength like that of using actual weapons.

Karate-dō is exercise through which the karateka masters all body movements by learning to move limbs and body backward and forward, left and right, up and down, freely and uniformly.

The techniques of karate-dō are well controlled according to the karateka's will power and are directed at the target accurately and spontaneously.

The essence of karate techniques is *kime*. The meaning of *kime* is an explosive attack to the target using the appropriate technique and maximum power in the shortest possible time. (Long ago, there was the expression *ikken hissatsu*, meaning "to kill with one blow," but to assume from this that killing is the objective is dangerous and incorrect. It should be remembered that the karateka of old were able to practice *kime* daily and in dead seriousness by using the makiwara.)

Kime may be accomplished by striking, punching or kicking, but also by blocking. A technique lacking *kime* is never true karate. A contest is no exception; however, it is against the rules to make contact because of the danger involved.

Sun-dome means to arrest a technique just before contact with the target (one *sun* is about three centimeters). But executing a technique without *kime* is not true karate, so the question is how to reconcile the contradiction between *kime* and *sun-dome*. The answer is this: establish the target slightly in front of the opponent's vital point. It can then be hit in a controlled way with maximum power without making contact.

Training transforms parts of the body into weapons to be used freely and effectively. The quality necessary to accomplish this is self-control. To become a victor, one must first overcome his own self.

KATA

The *kata* of karate-dō are logical arrangements of blocking, punching, striking and kicking techniques in certain set sequences. About fifty kata ("formal exercises") are practiced at the present time, some having been passed down from generation to generation, others being developed fairly recently.

Kata can be divided into two broad categories. In one group are those appropriate for physical development, the strengthening of bone and muscle. Seemingly simple, these kata require composure for their performance and exhibit strength and dignity when performed correctly. In the other group are kata suitable for developing fast reflexes and the ability to move quickly. The lightninglike movements in these kata are suggestive of the rapid flight of the swallow. All kata require and enhance rhythm and coordination.

Training in kata is spiritual as well as physical. In his performance of the kata, the karateka should exhibit boldness and confidence but also humility, gentleness and a sense of decorum, thus integrating mind and body in a singular discipline. As Gichin Funakoshi often reminded his students, "The spirit of karate-dō is lost without courtesy."

One expression of this courtesy is the bow made at the beginning and end of each kata. The stance is *musubi-dachi*, with the arms relaxed, hands lightly touching the thighs and eyes focused straight ahead.

After the bow, the karateka moves into the *kamae* of the first movement of the kata. This is a relaxed position devoid of tenseness, especially in the shoulders and knees, and breathing should be relaxed. The center of power and concentration is the *tanden*, the center of gravity. In this position, one should be full of fighting spirit and ready for any eventuality.

Being relaxed but alert also characterizes the bow completing the kata. This state is called *zanshin.* In karate-dō, as in other martial arts, bringing the kata to a perfect finish is of the greatest importance.

Each kata begins with a blocking technique and has a specific number of movements to be performed in a set order. There is some variation in the complexity of movements and the time required to complete them, but each has its own meaning and function and nothing is superfluous. Performance is carried out along the *embusen* ("performance line"), the shape of which is predetermined for each kata.

While performing a kata, the karateka should imagine being surrounded by enemies and be prepared to execute defensive and offensive techniques in any direction.

Mastery of kata is a prerequisite for advancement through *kyū* and *dan*. The kata in volumes 9, 10 and 11 of this series belong to the category of free kata, which may be selected for examination above 1st *dan*. They are kata of a fairly advanced level, and successful performance depends on having first mastered fundamentals, basic techniques and the required kata.

Important Points

Since the effects of practice are cumulative, train every day, even if only for a few minutes. When performing a kata, keep calm; never rush through the movements. This means always being aware of the correct timing of each movement. If a particular kata proves difficult, give it more attention, and always keep in mind the relationship between kata practice and kumite. (*See* Vols. 3 and 4.)

Specific points in performance are:

1. *Correct order.* The number and sequence of movements is predetermined. All must be performed.

2. *Beginning and end.* The kata must begin and end at the same spot on the *embusen.* This requires practice.

3. *Meaning of each movement.* Each movement, defensive or offensive, must be clearly understood and fully expressed. This is also true of a kata as a whole, since each one has its own characteristics.

4. *Awareness of the target.* The karateka must know what the target is and precisely when to execute a technique.

5. *Rhythm and timing.* Rhythm must be appropriate to the particular kata and the body must be flexible, never overstrained. Always keep in mind three factors: correct use of power, swiftness or slowness in executing techniques, and the stretching and contraction of muscles.

6. *Proper breathing.* Breathing should adjust to changing situations, but basically inhale when blocking, exhale when executing a finishing technique, and inhale and exhale while executing successive techniques.

Closely related to breathing is the *kiai* coming in the middle or at the end of the kata, at the moment of maximum tension. By exhaling very sharply and tensing the abdomen, extra power can be imparted to the muscles.

Standardization

The basic Heian and Tekki kata and the free kata from Bassai to Jion are all the essentially important Shōto-kan kata. In 1948, disciples from Keio, Waseda and Takushoku universities met with Master Gichin Funakoshi at Waseda University. Their purpose was to form a viewpoint for the unification of the kata, which in the period after the war had been subject to varied individual and subjective interpretations. The kata as presented in *Best Karate* embody the criteria for standardization established at that time.

Rhythm

BASSAI SHO

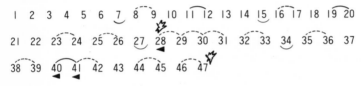

KANKŪ SHO

CHINTE

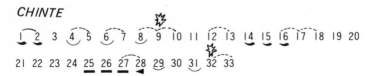

continuous, fast	—	powerfully
strong, continuous, fast		slow, powerfully
strong		*kiai*
increasingly strong		

14

Bassai Sho

Yōi

Shizen-tai to *musubi-dachi* to *heisoku-dachi*. After bowing, take *heisoku-dachi* and open both hands. Place left palm (palm to the right) vertically on right palm (palm

---

1a Ryō shō de kōhō o harau

Ryō kō soto muki

Side block against rear attack with both hands   Pivot left on left sole. Take a double step forward with right foot, side block rear attack with right palm.

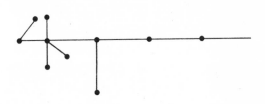

Heisoku-dachi

to the left) in front of lower abdomen.

1b	*Ryō shō jōdan yoko barai*

Ryō kō ushiro muki
Shōmen muki hanmi

Migi ashi mae kōsa-dachi

Upper level side block with both hands   Align left palm against back of right hand
(palms outward), block with back of hands.

2a

Migi shō hitai mae ni kazasu
Hidari shō hidari koshi mae

Migi kokō mae muki/Kō ushiro naname
shita muki/Hidari kō shita muki

Right hand in front of forehead/Left hand at left hip Bring both hands toward left side as if blocking a stick diagonally. Distance between the hands, about 60cm.

3a

Migi maeude gedan sukui uke

Kō naname shita muki

Right forearm downward scooping block Pivot on right leg, rotate hips rightward. While bringing right foot back to left foot, execute block in a semicircle.

2b *Hidari te hidari kata mae*
Migi shō migi kata ue

Hidari hiji yaya mageru
Tekubi o kaeshi kō ue muki

Migi kōkutsu-dachi

Left arm straight out from left shoulder/Right hand over right shoulder Perform *a* and *b* as one continuous movement, slowly but gradually increasing power.

3b *Migi gedan barai*

Kō naname ue muki

Heisoku-dachi

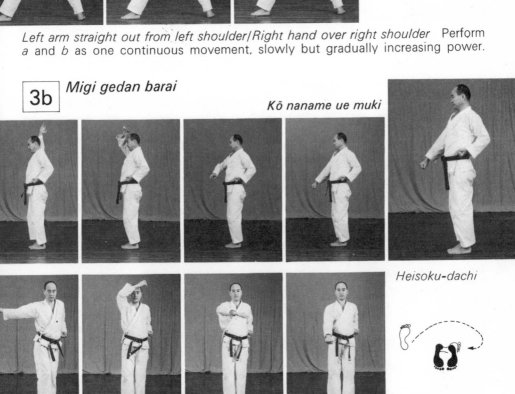

Right downward block Swing right fist up and strike diagonally downward from above the head in a large circular motion to the left.

4 | *Ryō shō bō uke*

Two-handed stick block   Slide left foot forward into right back stance. This technique is like Movement 2.

5 | *Migi shō o hidari ken ue ni kasaneru* *Migi kō shita muki/Hidari*
       Hidari ken hidari koshi kamae   *kō shita muki/Shōmen muki*

Heisoku-dachi

Right hand on left fist/Left fist at left hip   Pivot on right leg, rotate hips leftward and pull the left foot back.

Hidari muki hanmi

Migi kōkutsu-dachi

---

6 *Migi haitō migi yoko jōdan yoko uchi*
Migi sokutō yoko keage   *Kō shita muki*

Hidari ashi-dachi

Upper level right ridge hand strike to right side/Right side snap kick with right sword foot

21

7 | *Hidari tate shutō chūdan yoko uke*
Migi ken migi koshi ni kaikomu

Middle level block to side with left vertical sword hand/Right fist return to right side Put kicking leg down and bring left hand to the front in an arclike motion

8 | *Migi chūdan-zuki*

Right middle level straight punch

Kiba-dachi

Hiji nobashi tekubi tateru

Kiba-dachi

from under right elbow.

<table>
</table>

9 | *Hidari chūdan-zuki*

Kiba-dachi

Left middle level straight punch

10

Migi ken migi yoko jōdan uchi uke
Hidari ken hidari yoko gedan uke

Upper level block, inside outward, to right side with right fist/Lower level block to left side with left fist   Pivot on right leg, rotate hips leftward.   Open right hand

11

Hidari ken hidari yoko jōdan uchi uke
Migi ken migi yoko gedan uke

Upper level block, inside outward, to left side with left fist/Lower level block to right side with right fist   Twist hips sharply. The essential points are the same as

Shōmen muki/Kao hidari muki

Migi kōkutsu-dachi

and bring it strongly from under left elbow back above right side while clenching fist. Right elbow at shoulder level. (*cf.* Jitte 19, Jion 18)

Shōmen muki/Kao migi muki

Hidari kōkutsu-dachi

in Movement 10.

12 | *Migi shutō uke*

Right sword hand block   Pivot on left leg, rotate hips leftward. Slide right foot forward.

13 | *Hidari shutō uke*

Shōmen muki hanmi

Migi kōkutsu-dachi

Left sword hand block   Slide left foot forward.

14 | *Migi shutō uke*

Right sword hand block

Shōmen muki hanmi

Hidari kōkutsu-dachi

| 15 | *Hidari shutō uke* |

Shōmen muki hanmi

Shōmen muki hanmi

Hidari kōkutsu-dachi

Migi kōkutsu-dachi

Slide right foot forward.   *Left sword hand block* Pull right foot back.

16 | *Ryō shō tsukami uke*

Grasping block with both hands Rotate hips leftward keeping feet in place. Describe arc to the front with right hand from under left elbow. Both palms down-

17 | *Ryō shō tsukami yose*
Migi sokutō gedan kekomi

Grasping-pulling with both palms/Lower level thrust kick with right sword foot Clench both fists and pull them strongly toward the right side of the chest. Raise

Hidari zenkutsu-dachi

ward. This is the same as Bassai Dai 18, 19.

Hidari ashi-dachi

right knee chest high (between extended arms).

29

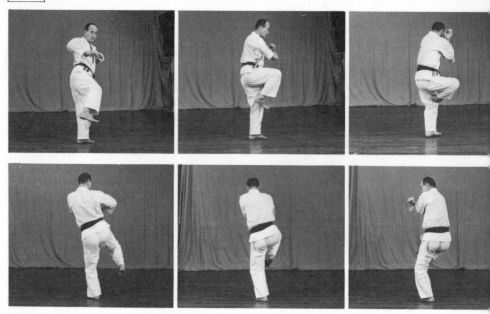

Middle level reverse wedge block After thrust kick, put right foot down and simultaneously rotate hips leftward. Block on reversing direction of torso.

19 *Ryō ken chūdan-zuki*

Middle level double-fist punch Keeping the stance, slide feet forward while punching. Pull fists back immediately.

Hiji mage/Ryō kō shita muki
Ushiro muki

Migi kōkutsu-dachi

Kō shita muki

Migi kōkutsu-dachi

20a *Migi ken o hidari ken no ue ni kasaneru*

Right fist on left fist Bring right fist in a circular motion to left hip as if blocking an upper level attack, while pulling left fist to left hip. Rotate leftward.

21 *Hidari shutsui hidari yoko chūdan uchi*
Migi ken migi koshi kamae

Kiba-dachi

Left middle level hammer-fist strike to left side/Right fist at right hip Bring left hammer-fist from under right arm. Rotate right fist while pulling it back to right hip.

20b
Migi ken migi yoko chūdan-zuki (*Tsuki uke*)
Hidari ken migi yoko chūdan-zuki

Kiba-dachi

Right middle level punch to right side (*punching block*) / *Left middle level punch to right side*   Step right on right foot. Punch with both fists simultaneously.

22   **Migi chūdan oi-zuki**

*Migi
zenkutsu-dachi*

Right middle level lunge punch   Slide right foot forward.

23
Migi ken migi yoko chūdan-zuki
Hidari ken migi yoko chūdan-zuki

Right middle level punch to right side/Left middle level punch to right side   Rotate hips widely leftward with left leg as pivot.

24
Hidari ken hidari yoko chūdan-zuki
Migi ken hidari yoko chūdan-zuki

Left middle level punch to left side/Right middle level punch to left side   Rotate hips rightward with right leg as pivot.

Migi ken migi yoko chūdan-zuki (Tsuki uke)
Hidari ken migi yoko chūdan-zuki

Kiba-dachi

Right middle level punch to right side (punching block)/Left middle level punch to right side   Step right on right foot. Punch with both fists simultaneously.

22   *Migi chūdan oi-zuki*

Migi zenkutsu-dachi

Right middle level lunge punch   Slide right foot forward.

23 *Migi ken migi yoko chūdan-zuki*
Hidari ken migi yoko chūdan-zuki

Right middle level punch to right side / Left middle level punch to right side   Rotate hips widely leftward with left leg as pivot.

24 *Hidari ken hidari yoko chūdan-zuki*
Migi ken hidari yoko chūdan-zuki

Left middle level punch to left side / Right middle level punch to left side   Rotate hips rightward with right leg as pivot.

Kiba-dachi

Kiba-dachi

35

25 | Migi ken migi yoko chūdan-zuki
Hidari ken migi yoko chūdan-zuki

Right middle level punch to right side/Left middle level punch to right side Rotate hips leftward with left leg as pivot.

26 | Hidari shō chūdan tsukami uke
Migi shō gedan tsukami uke

Middle level grasping block with left hand/Lower level grasping block with right hand Raise left hand from under right arm in a high arc to come in front of left

Kiba-dachi

Ryō kō ue muki/Kokō tomo ni mae muki

*Hidari ashi mae
neko ashi-dachi*

snoulder. Swing right hand high above head and left shoulder, then downward toward left hip. Cross hands in front of face as if describing a mountain.

37

Migi shō chūdan tsukami yose
Hidari shō chūdan tsukami yose

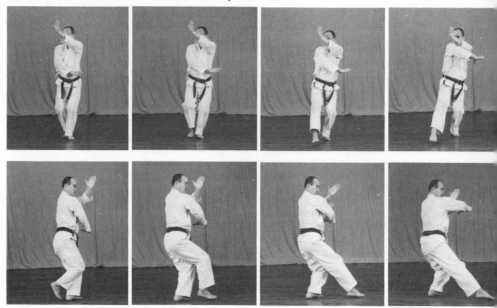

Middle level grasp-pull with right hand/Lower level grasp-pull with left hand
Move right foot in front of left foot with left foot as pivot, then transfer weight to

Naore

Bring right foot to left foot, return to *Yōi.*

Neko ashi-dachi

left leg. Take cat leg stance, right foot slowly describing an arc from the left. Face to right front.

Heisoku-dachi

BASSAI SHO: IMPORTANT POINTS

Bassai Sho should be practiced after mastering Bassai Dai. The two kata form a series, differing in the point that Bassai Dai outwardly shows power and solemnity while Bassai Sho, in the calmness of its techniques, contains an inner strength.

Characteristics of Bassai Sho include the arclike movements of hands and feet and the use of the sword hand, ridge hand and tiger mouth. The techniques learned in this kata are defence against stick attacks. The palm is often used for this purpose and strength is important for each block, especially against heavy sticks. Wrists, elbows and knees must be flexible and stances must be stable.

Of particular importance are the correct application of power and the appropriate speed in executing techniques. This is a good kata for learning how to block strongly and counterattack sharply after tensing muscles slowly in accordance with breathing.

Bassai Dai is presented in Vol. 6 of this series.

1. Movement 1. While preparing to step in to take care of the frontal attack, push aside the stick attack coming from the rear with both palm-heels placed together. Use both hands to block the upper level attack from the front.

41

2. Movement 2. This is a good block against a stick aimed at your head. With tiger mouths open and both palms facing up, catch and grasp the middle of the stick. Pull the right elbow backward, turning the wrist over as it passes in front of the forehead. Simultaneously, raise left hand and tighten the left side of the body.

3. Movement 3. To counter a kick from the side, swing the right hand widely from above the shoulder in coordination with the rightward rotation of the hips. Scoop the kick to the side with the thumb-side of the forearm. Follow through with a throw or a hammer fist strike to the side of the assailant's body.

4. Movement 19. In executing a reverse wedge block, there should be the feeling of pulling the assailant's arms toward the outside and toward yourself. After the block, close the distance by sliding the feet and straighten both elbows for a double-fisted close punch.

5. Movement 20. Block the opponent's upper level punch with the little-finger side of the right wrist by twisting the wrist while bringing the arm from directly above the left hip. Straighten the right elbow for the punching block. Simultaneously deliver a punch with the left fist to the solar plexus.

6. Movements 26/27. To counter a punch to your solar plexus coming from the left oblique, wheel both hands from over the head, grasp the assailant's wrist with the right hand and his elbow with the left hand. Move left foot outward in an arc and throw him off balance while hooking his ankle. Do the same against the assailant coming from the right side.

Kankū Sho

Yōi

1 | *Hidari morote chūdan uke*

Left middle level augmented forearm block Slide right foot half a step to right. Right fist at left elbow. Backs of fists downward.

Hachinoji-dachi

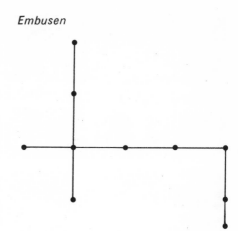

Hidari muki hanmi

Migi kōkutsu-dachi

2 *Migi morote chūdan uke*

Right middle level augmented forearm block   Slide feet to left.

3 *Hidari morote chūdan uke*

Left middle level augmented forearm block   Slide right foot back to take stance.

50

Migi muki hanmi

Hidari kōkutsu-dachi

Shōmen muki hanmi

Migi kōkutsu-dachi

4a | *Migi chūdan oi-zuki*

Right middle level lunge punch   Slide right foot one step forward.

4b | *Migi maeude hineri*

5a | *Hidari chūdan oi-zuki*

Migi zenkutsu-dachi

Twist right forearm   Relax elbow immediately. Tighten right side, naturally bringing elbow closer to body.

52

Migi zenkutsu-dachi

Hidari zenkutsu-dachi

Left middle level lunge punch

5b — Hidari maeude hineri

Hidari zenkutsu-dachi

Twist forearm Slide left foot one step forward. Same as Movement 4.

6 — Migi chūdan oi-zuki

Right middle level lunge punch

7 — Migi shō tsukami uke / Hidari shō migi tekubi o tsukamu

Grasping block with right palm/Hold right wrist with left hand Pivot on right leg, rotate hips leftward. Reverse direction quickly. Open right fist and bring it forward

54

Shōmen muki

Migi zenkutsu-dachi

Kokō hiraku
Ushiro muki gyaku hanmi

Hidari zenkutsu-dachi
(*yaya asaku*)

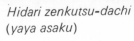

circularly from under left elbow in a grasping action. Use left hand to pull right wrist towards body.

55

8 Migi mae keage

Hidari ashi-dachi

Right front snap kick Execute while returning right elbow strongly to right side.

9

Migi uraken jōdan tate mawashi uchi
Hidari ken hidari koshi

Upper level vertical strike with right back-fist/Left fist at left side Bring left foot behind right ankle for stance.

Migi ashi mae kōsa-dachi

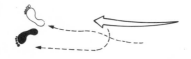

10 *Migi chūdan uchi uke*
Hidari ken hidari koshi

Kō shita muki
Ushiro muki hanmi

Right middle level block, inside outward/Left fist at left side Bring left foot back a step. Keep right elbow in place, return right fist from under left arm to the right,

12 *Migi chūdan-zuki*
Hidari ken hidari koshi

13 *Migi ken migi yoko*
chūdan uchi uke

Migi zenkutsu-dachi

Right middle level punch/Left fist at left side
Movements 11 and 12 are alternate punching.

58

Migi zenkutsu-dachi

Migi zenkutsu-dachi

elbow bent, forearm slanting upward.

Left middle level punch/Right fist at right side

Hidari ken zenpō gedan-barai

Shōmen muki hanmi

Migi kōkutsu-dachi

Right middle level block, inside outward, with right fist/Left fist downward block to front   Pivot on right leg, rotate hips leftward. Reverse direction quickly.

14 | *Hidari ken furioroshi uchi*
Migi ken migi koshi

Left fist downward swinging strike/Right fist at right side　Bring left fist to right shoulder and make a loop from the chin, swinging downward to strike with

15 | *Migi shō tsukami uke*
Hidari shō migi tekubi o tsukamu

Grasping block with right palm/Hold right wrist with left hand　Same as Movement 7.

60

Kō ue muki
Shōmen muki hanmi

Hidari mae renoji-dachi

the second row of knuckles.

Shōmen muki
gyaku hanmi

Hidari zenkutsu-dachi

61

Hidari ashi-dachi

Right front snap kick   Same as Movement 8.

Kō shita muki
Shōmen muki hanmi

18 *Migi chūdan uchi uke*

Kōsa-dachi

Upper level vertical strike with right back-fist
Same as Movement 9.

Migi uraken jōdan tate mawashi uchi

Kō shita muki
Shōmen muki hanmi

Migi zenkutsu-dachi

Right middle level block, inside outward Bring left foot back a step. Same as Movement 10.

19 | *Hidari chūdan-zuki*

Left middle level punch

Migi zenkutsu-dachi

21 | *Migi ken migi yoko chūdan uchi uke*
Hidari ken zenpō gedan-barai

Right middle level block, inside outward, with right fist/Left fist downward block to front Pivot on left leg, rotate hips leftward. Reverse direction quickly. Same as

64

Migi chūdan-zuki

Migi zenkutsu-dachi

Right middle level punch   Movements 19 and 20 are alternate punching.

Ushiro muki

Migi kōkutsu-dachi

Movement 13.

22 | Hidari ken furioroshi uchi
Migi ken migi koshi

Left fist downward swinging strike/Right fist at right side   Same as Movement 14.

23 | Migi ken migi yoko jōdan uchi uke
Hidari ken hidari yoko gedan uke

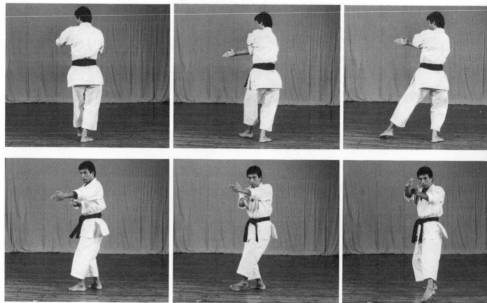

Right upper level block, inside outward, with right fist/Left lower level block with left fist   Pivot on right leg, rotate hips leftward. Open and clench right fist while

66

Hiji nobashi kō ue muki
Ushiro muki hanmi

Hidari mae renoji-dachi

Ushiro muki/Kao hidari muki

Migi kōkutsu-dachi

pulling it from under left elbow to upper right side.

67

24 | *Hidari ken hidari yoko chūdan-zuki*
Migi ken hidari yoko chūdan-zuki

Left middle level punch with left fist/Left middle level punch with right fist Slide feet leftward. Swing left fist to the right and using this reaction thrust both fists

25 | *Hidari ken hidari yoko jōdan uchi uke*
Migi gedan barai

Left upper level block, inside outward, with left fist/Right lower level block with right fist

Ushiro muki/Kao hidari muki

Kiba-dachi

simultaneously to left side making arms parallel.

Ushiro muki/Kao migi muki

Hidari kōkutsu-dachi

Migi ken migi yoko chūdan-zuki
Hidari ken migi yoko chūdan-zuki

Right middle level punch with right fist/Right middle level punch with left fist
Same as Movement 24.

Ryō shō bō uke

Two-handed stick block Bring left foot half a step rightward to support body
weight, rotate hips leftward while sliding right foot one step forward. Open right

Ushiro muki/Kao migi muki

Kiba-dachi

Ushiro muki hanmi

Hidari kōkutsu-dachi

palm, bring it circularly in front of right hip with elbow stretched a little, palm upward. Bring left palm, slanting upward, in front of forehead.

Migi kō ue muki
Hidari kō shita muki
Ushiro muki hanmi

Push right fist diagonally downward/Left fist in front of right side Slide feet slightly forward. Clench both fists and strongly push diagonally downward while

Jump with 360° turn Jump high, fold legs, and turn 360° leftward. Jump must be at least 40 to 50 cm to escape having legs swept by stick.

72

29a · *Tobiagari ichi kaiten*

Hidari kōkutsu-dachi

twisting wrists.

29b · *Migi shutō chūdan uke*

Hidari kōkutsu-dachi

Right middle level sword hand block   Block must be completed on landing.

30 *Hidari uraken jōdan yoko mawashi uchi*
Hidari yoko keage/Migi ken migi koshi

Upper level horizontal strike with left back-fist/Left side snap kick/Right fist at right side

31 *Migi empi uchi*

Right elbow strike Immediately after left foot is on the ground, strike left palm with right elbow.

Ushiro muki
Kao hidari muki

Migi ashi-dachi

Hidari muki

Hidari zenkutsu-dachi

32 | Migi uraken jōdan yoko mawashi uchi / Migi yoko keage / Hidari ken hidari koshi

Upper level horizontal strike with right back-fist/Right side snap kick/Left fist at left side

33 | Hidari empi uchi
Migi muki

Migi zenkutsu-dachi

Left elbow strike   Strike right palm.

34 | Migi shō tsukami uke / Hidari shō migi tekubi

Grasping block with right palm/Hold right wrist with left hand

Ushiro muki/Kao migi muki

Hidari ashi-dachi

o tsukamu

Kokō hiraku
Ushiro muki gyaku hanmi

Hidari zenkutsu-dachi

77

Right front snap kick

Ushiro muki hanmi

Migi ashi mae kōsa-dachi

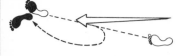

Upper level vertical strike with right back-fist Pivot on left leg, take a full step forward with right foot. Bring left foot behind right ankle for stance.

Migi uraken jōdan tate mawashi uchi

Hidari ashi-dachi

37 *Migi chūdan uchi uke*

Ushiro muki hanmi

Migi zenkutsu-dachi

Right middle level block, inside outward Bring left foot back a step.

Migi zenkutsu-dachi

Left middle level punch   *Right middle level punch*

Movements 38 and 39 are alternate punching.

foot, striking left palm while in a low jump.

40 | *Mikazuki-geri*

Crescent kick   Keep right front stance, rotate hips leftward. While turning head to left, stretch left palm backward at shoulder level. Deliver crescent kick with right

41 | *Fuse no shisei*
Tsumasaki-dachi kakato ukasu

Migi ashi mae hikui zenkutsu-dachi

Going to ground position   Immediately after crescent kick, rotate hips sharply leftward. Stretch left leg backward while body is still in the air.

81

Ushiro muki hanmi

Lower level left sword hand block   Take stance by switching position of feet.

Ushiro muki hanmi

Right middle level sword hand block   Slide right foot forward.

Migi kōkutsu-dachi (*hikume*)

Hidari kōkutsu-dachi

44 | *Hidari chūdan uchi uke*

Left middle level block, inside outward Pivot on right leg, rotate hips leftward.

45 | *Migi chūdan oi-zuki*

Right middle level lunge punch Slide right foot forward.

Migi muki hanmi

Hidari zenkutsu-dachi

Migi muki

Migi zenkutsu-dachi

46 | *Migi chūdan uchi uke*

Right middle level block, inside outward   Pivot on left leg, rotate hips rightward.

47 | *Hidari chūdan oi-zuki*

Hidari muki

Naore

Hidari zenkutsu-dachi

Left middle level lunge punch
Slide right foot forward.

Hidari muki hanmi

Migi zenkutsu-dachi

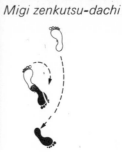

Hachinoji-dachi

Rotate hips leftward and withdraw left leg to return to posture of *Yōi*.

KANKŪ SHO: IMPORTANT POINTS

Before practicing Kankū Sho, the fundamentals in Heian 4 must be thoroughly learned. It should not be practiced until all the techniques in Kankū Dai have been mastered. The configuration of offensive and defensive techniques in the two kata is almost the same, as are the speed and sharpness of rotation and various techniques. The difference is found in the counter-attacks making use of the sword hand strike or front kick after a block. In Kankū Dai, these are delivered mainly to the upper level, in Kankū Sho, mainly to the middle level.

In performing this kata, remember to express three factors: correct use of power, speed of techniques, and the stretching and contraction of muscles. Kankū Sho cannot be mastered until the karateka has fully understood that the high jump and low turn are not a single action.

1. Movement 4. It is incorrect to execute the middle level block from inside outward after punching. The correct way is, after punching with explosive force, to immediately relax the elbow and rotate the forearm.

A karateka cannot be called a true expert until he masters this punch. It should not be executed using only pushing power. The spring and flexibility of the elbow must be given full expression.

As seen in the illustrations, when the wrist is captured after punching, quickly and strongly pull back and twist to release it.

The important point is to relax the elbow momentarily right after punching, which will make it possible to turn the wrist naturally and recapture the arm. Do not pull the elbow outward. Bring it back to the side of the stomach. (*See also* Vol. 8, p. 141.)

2. Movement 7. Open the right hand and describe an arc forward from under the left hand as if to grasp something. Grip the right wrist with the left hand. Keep thumb and other fingers together.

From a strong and stable half-front facing stance, seize the assailant and pull back with both hands. Bring the right fist toward the right side of the stomach.

3. Movements 13/14. After the right middle level block with the right forearm and the left downward block, raise the left fist forcefully straight above the right shoulder, slightly withdrawing the front foot. Immediately strike down to the middle level in front, describing a small arc.

This movement also has the meaning of releasing the captured left wrist. See next page for application.

4. Movements 13/14. The above photos show the application of Movements 13 and 14 in kumite. When striking, use the second row of left knuckles and strike the opponent's punching hand or chest.

5. Movements 23/24. After the upper level side block, strike the opponent's solar plexus with the right fist while sliding the feet to the left. Immediately rotate the hips to shift the body to the right and deliver a blocking punch with the right arm against the opponent's punching arm. At the same time, strike his solar plexus with the left fist.

6. Movements 28/29. Block the downward swinging stick with both hands and push hard diagonally downward to throw the opponent off balance. Counter a second stick attack coming from the rear to sweep your legs by jumping and turning leftward. On landing attack with sword hand to the side of the head of the opponent on the right.

Rather than the height of the jump, the important point is to bend and hold the knees close to the chest.

7. Movements 40/41. Turning the head back, block the opponent's punch with the left hand and deliver a middle level crescent kick. Immediately make another half turn of the body by going to ground to avoid the opponent's attack. Do this by thrusting the left foot backward—after kicking but before the kicking foot hits the ground—while turning the body in the air close to the ground. Hands and feet land at the same time. Note the importance of keeping the jump low.

Chinte

Yōi

Fists in front of solar plexus *kamae.* Right fist (back forward) on top of left fist (back downward).

1 *Migi kentsui chūdan tate mawashi uchi*
Hidari ken suigetsu mae kamae

Right middle level hammer fist vertical strike/Left fist in front of chest kamae
Slowly raise right hammer fist high in front of forehead, then strike down to

98

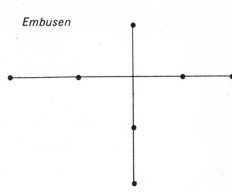

Embusen

Heisoku-dachi

Hidari kō shita muki

Heisoku-dachi

shoulder level, gradually increasing power.

2 | *Hidari kentsui chūdan tate mawashi uchi*
Migi ken suigetsu mae kamae

Left middle level vertical hammer fist strike/Right fist in front of chest kamae

Slowly raise left hammer fist in front of forehead, gradually increasing power, then strike down to left shoulder level. Movements 1 and 2 must be done slowly and con-

Migi kō shita muki

Heisoku-dachi

tinuously without any pause in breathing.

3 | *Ryō shō jōdan age-uke*

Upper level rising block with sword hands   Pivot on right leg, slide left foot forward and rotate hips rightward. Simultaneously, raise both sword hands in front

4 | *Migi chūdan tate shutō uke*

Right middle level vertical sword hand block   Pivot on left leg, slide right foot slightly rightward. Right hand and right foot move simultaneously and slowly.

Migi te mae/Ryō kō uchi muki

Kiba-dachi

of forehead until index and middle fingers touch.

Migi fudō-dachi

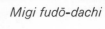

5 *Hidari chūdan tate-zuki*

Left middle level vertical punch Keeping same position of feet, strongly straighten knee of back leg and push hips to rotate. Counterattack with reverse punch. (Strike

6 *Hidari chūdan tate shutō uke*

Left middle level vertical sword hand block Pivot on right leg, slide left foot slightly forward. Left hand and left foot move simultaneously and slowly.

Migi zenkutsu-dachi

right palm with left fist.) Movements 4 and 5 should be performed as slow block and fast punch.

Hidari fudō-dachi

7 | *Migi chūdan tate-zuki*

Right middle level vertical punch Change from rooted stance to front stance to execute right vertical-fist punch. Strike left palm with right fist.

8 | *Migi chūdan tate shutō uke*

Right middle level vertical sword hand block

Hidari zenkutsu-dachi

Migi fudō-dachi

9 | *Hidari jōdan tate empi uchi*

Left upper level vertical elbow strike   Change from rooted stance to front stance to deliver upward elbow strike to face. (Strike right palm with left elbow.)

10 | *Hidari chūdan shutō uke*

Left middle level sword hand block

Migi zenkutsu-dachi

Migi kōkutsu-dachi

11 | Migi chūdan shutō uke

Right middle level sword hand block   Pivot on left leg, slide right foot forward while executing the sword hand block.

12 | Hidari chūdan mae-geri

Ryō te Kyodō 11 no mama

Left middle level front kick/Hands in same position as in Movement 11

Hidari kōkutsu-dachi

Migi ashi-dachi

13 | Migi chūdan uchi uke
Hidari gedan uke

Migi
zenkutsu-dachi

Right middle level block, inside outward/Left downward block

14 | Migi gedan uchi uke

Right lower level block, inside outward Slide left foot toward right foot to take

15 | Hidari gedan haitō mawashi uke
Migi te suigetsu mae ni kamaeru

Left downward ridge hand block/Right hand in front of chest kamae Pivot on left leg, rotate hips rightward, and slide right foot to the right to take stance. Simulta-

Heisoku-daohi

stance. Turn right wrist over while blocking. Continue to swing right hand in a large circle, passing over the head and stopping in front of the lower abdomen.

Migi kō shita muki

Kiba-dachi

neously move both hands in a large arc from the left side, hands almost parallel.

Migi gedan haitō mawashi uke
Hidari te suigetsu mae ni kamaeru

Right downward ridge hand block/Left hand in front of chest kamae

Ryō ken chūdan kakiwake

Middle level reverse wedge block

Hidari kō shita muki

Kiba-dachi

Ryō kō shita muki

Kiba-dachi

Ryō ken gedan-gamae
Migi ashikō hidari hiza ura ni soeru

Fists out to sides downward kamae   Bring right instep against back of left knee.
Do Movements 16, 17 and 18 continuously and fast.

Hidari ashi-dachi

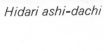

19 | *Migi nakadaka ippon ken chūdan uchi otoshi*

Middle level falling block with right one-knuckle fist

20 | *Hidari nakadaka ippon ken chūdan uchi otoshi*
Migi ken Kyodō 19 no mama

Middle level falling block with left one-knuckle fist Keep right fist in same position as in Movement 19.

Migi zenkutsu-dachi

Migi zenkutsu-dachi

21 *Nihon nukite migi chūdan uchi uke*

Right middle level two-finger spear hand block, inside outward Keeping front stance, rotate hips leftward while bringing right arm from under left elbow.

22 *Hidari nihon nukite jōdan age-zuki*

Upper level rising punch with left two-finger spear hand

Migi zenkutsu-dachi

Hidari zenkutsu-dachi

23 *Nihon nukite hidari chūdan uchi uke*

Left middle level two-finger spear hand block, inside outward Pivot on right leg
and withdraw left foot while rotating hips leftward.

24 *Migi nihon nukite jōdan age-zuki*

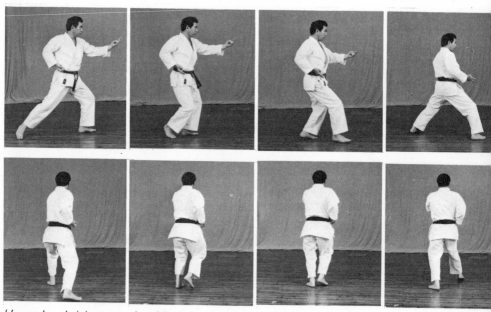

Upper level rising punch with right two-finger spear hand

Hidari zenkutsu-dachi

Migi zenkutsu-dachi

Migi teishō chūdan soto mawashi uke

Right middle level roundhouse palm-heel block, outside inward   Pivot on left leg, rotate hips leftward.

Hidari teishō chūdan soto mawashi uchi

Middle level roundhouse strike, outside inward, with left palm-heel/Right hand same position as in Movement 25.

Migi fudō-dachi

Migi fudō-dachi

125

27 *Ryō ken ryō gawa e hikiharau*

Both fists out to sides

28 *Ryō ken chūdan hasami-zuki*

Middle level scissors punch   Pivot on right leg, rotate hips quickly leftward, and face to the front. Movements 27 and 28 must be done continuously and quickly.

Migi fudō-dachi

Hidari fudō-dachi

127

29 *Migi chūdan tate shutō uke*

Right vertical sword hand block

30 *Hidari chūdan tate-zuki*

Left middle level vertical punch   Strike right palm with left fist.

Migi fudō-dachi

Migi zenkutsu-dachi

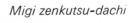

129

31 *Hidari chūdan tate shutō uke*

Left middle level vertical sword hand block

32 *Migi chūdan tate-zuki*

Right middle level vertical punch

Hidari fudō-dachi

Hidari zenkutsu-dachi

Strike left palm with right fist.

131

Right fist in front of chest/Left palm wrapped around right fist On completion of
vertical fist punch, take three small jumping steps backward, aligning left foot with

Naore

Heisoku-dachi

right foot on first step, then moving feet in unison.

Hachinoji-dachi

133

CHINTE: IMPORTANT POINTS

The name *Chinte,* written with Chinese characters indicating "extraordinary" and "hand," is thought to derive from the unique techniques in the kata. The kata as a whole has a sequence of movements beginning in tranquility, becoming powerful and ending in calmness.

There is much to learn from this kata. One point is the acquisition of the technique of punching employing power generated by pushing the back foot against the ground. After blocking in the rooted stance, the rear knee is pushed forward to take the front stance.

Another point is the *tateken,* rarely seen in basic karate techniques, though it is common in Chinese martial arts. There are also techniques for attacking the eyes with the two-finger spear hand. This is effective self-defense for women who lack strong muscular power.

The last movement requires the feeling of strength in calmness, of waves quietly receding after dashing hard against the shore.

1. Movements 1/2. Swing the right arm in a wide motion passing in front of the face to the right. Strike with the hammer fist against the opponent's punching arm or collarbone. Immediately turn head to the left and counterattack in that direction with the same technique. These two actions are done in one breath.

2. Movement 3. Raise both hands in front of the forehead and bring the fingers together. Put the right palm on the back of the left hand and lightly touch tips of index and middle fingers. In executing this block, the hands extend the body's center line upward. To weaken the opponent's power, pull the blocking hands slightly toward you.

3. Movements 9/10. After the upward elbow strike to the chin, rotate hips sharply to the left with right foot as pivot while executing left sword hand block. Shift right front stance to right back stance without changing position of right knee.

4. Movement 14. Against a kick from the front, swing the arm down widely, turning the wrist inward, and block with the thumb-side of the forearm. Continue the wide upward swinging motion and upset the opponent's balance. During this action, bring the rear foot to the front foot to take the feet-together stance.

5. Movement 15. Block the kicking attack from the left with the left ridge hand and swing both hands high overhead to put the assailant off balance.

6. Movement 16. Against a kick and a punch coming from the right side, block the kick with the right ridge hand and grasp the assailant's punching arm with the left hand. Pulling the left elbow toward the side of the stomach, swing the right ridge hand upward. (Note the similarity to application of Movement 15.) This action should cause the opponent to fall down.

The arms are swung in a way similar to the shoulder wheel (*kata-guruma*) throw of Judo.

7. Movement 18. Assume that after the middle level reverse wedge block you are attacked from the front with a stick or by kicking. Since there is no time to dodge the attack, quickly raise the right foot behind the left knee to take the one-legged stance and execute the downward block.

8. Movement 22. The two-finger spear hand attack to the eyes does not require strong power. The important point is the course the hand takes. It should describe a semicircle coming up from a low position to hit the target.

9. Movements 26/27. To counter a frontal punching attack, strike the opponent's inner wrist hard with the palm-heel. Simultaneously deliver a hard strike with the left palm-heel to the elbow. Grab his wrist with the right hand and pull strongly to the right rear. It is important to fully bend and tighten the wrist.

10. Movement 28. Against a middle level attack from behind, rotate the hips leftward with right foot as pivot and execute the scissors punch to the sides of your assailant's body. Drop the hips very low for maximum effectiveness.

GLOSSARY

age-uke, rising block
age-zuki, rising punch
ashi, foot, leg
ashiko, instep

bō, stick

chichi, nipple
chūdan, middle level
chūdan uchi, middle level
  strike
chūdan-zuki, middle level
  punch

embusen, performance line
empi, elbow
empi uchi, elbow strike

fudō-dachi, rooted stance
furioroshi uchi, downward
  swinging strike
fuse no shisei, going-to-
  ground position

gawa, side
gedan, lower level
gedan barai, downward
  block
gedan uke, lower level block
gyaku hanmi, reverse half-
  front facing

hachinoji-dachi, open-leg
  stance
haitō, ridge hand
hanmi, half-front facing
harau, parry
hasami-zuki, scissors punch
heisoku-dachi, feet-together
  stance
hidari, left
hiji, elbow
hikiharau, clear away
hikiyose, pull near

hikui, low
hineri, twist, turn
hiraku, open
hitai, forehead
hiza, knee

ichi, one
ikken hissatsu, to kill with one
  blow

jōdan, upper level

kabuseru, wrap
kaikomu, hold (under the
  arm)
kaiten, turn
kakato, heel
kakiwake uke, reverse wedge
  block
kamae, posture, position
kao, face
karuku, lightly
kasaneru, pile up
kata, shoulder
kata-guruma, shoulder wheel
kazasu, hold aloft
keage, snap kick
kekomi, thrust kick
ken, fist
kentsui uchi, hammer fist
  strike
kiba-dachi, straddle-leg
  stance
kimi, decide
kō, back of fist
kōhō, back direction
kokō, tiger mouth
kōkutsu-dachi, back stance
kōsa-dachi, crossed-feet
  stance
koshi, hip
kyodō, movement

mae, front, in front of

mae keage, front snap kick
maeude, forearm, wrist
mageru, bend
mama, as it is
mawashi uchi, roundhouse strike
mawashi uke, roundhouse block
migi, right
migi ashi-dachi, right leg stance
migi ashi mae, right leg in front
mikazuki-geri, crescent kick
morote, both hands
morote uke, augmented block
mune, chest
musubi-dachi, informal attention stance, toes out

nakadaka ippon ken, one knuckle fist
naname, diagonally, obliquely
naore, return to *yōi*
neko ashi-dachi, cat leg stance
nihon nukite, two-finger spear hand
nobashi, straighten, extend

oi-zuki, lunge punch
oshinobasu, push-extend
otoshi, falling

renoji-dachi, L stance
ryō, both

sahō, left direction
shita muki, facing downward
shita ni, down
shizen-tai, natural position
shō, palm
shōmen, front
shōmen muki, facing to the front
shutō, sword hand
shutō uke, sword hand block
shutsui, hammer fist
soeru, attach
sokumen, side
sokutō, sword foot
soto, outside-inward
soto muki, facing outward
suigetsu, solar plexus

sukui uke, scooping block
sun, unit of length, about three centimeters
sun-dome, to arrest a technique just before making contact
suri-ashi, sliding the feet

tanden, center of gravity
tateken, vertical fist
tate mawashi uchi, vertical roundhouse strike
tateru, raise
tate shutō, vertical sword hand
tate-zuki, vertical punch
te, hand
teishō. palm-heel
tekubi, wrist, forearm
tobiagari, jump
tomo ni, together
tsukami uke, grasping block
tsukami yose, grasping-pulling
tsukamu, grasp
tsuki uke, strike-block
tsumasaki-dachi, tip-toe stance

uchi, strike
uchi uke, inside-outward block
ue, up, on top of
ue muki, facing upward
uhō, right direction
ukasu, float
uke, block
ura, back side
uraken, back-fist
ushiro muki, facing to the back

yaya, slightly
yaya asaku, slightly shallow
yōi, position of readiness
yoko, side
yoko barai, side block
yoko keage, side snap kick
yoko uchi, strike to side
yoko uke, sideward block

zanshin, relaxed but alert state of readiness
zenkutsu-dachi, front stance
zenpō, front direction